Tackling Interview Questions
in a week

MO SHAPIRO
ALISON STRAW

Hodder & Stoughton

A MEMBER OF THE HODDER HEADLINE GROUP

Orders: please contact Bookpoint Ltd, 130 Milton Park, Abingdon, Oxon OX14 4SB.
Telephone: (44) 01235 827720, Fax: (44) 01235 400454. Lines are open from 9.00–6.00, Monday to Saturday, with a 24 hour message answering service.
Email address: orders@bookpoint.co.uk

British Library Cataloguing in Publication Data
A catalogue record for this title is available from The British Library

ISBN 0 340 849487

First published	1999
Impression number	10 9 8 7 6 5 4 3 2 1
Year	2007 2006 2005 2003 2002

Typeset by SX Composing DTP, Rayleigh, Essex.
Printed in Great Britain for Hodder & Stoughton Educational, a division of Hodder Headline Plc, 338 Euston Road, London NW1 3BH by Cox & Wyman Ltd, Reading, Berkshire.

■■■ C O N T E N T S ■■■

■■■ I N T R O D U C T I O N ■■■

Since writing *Succeeding at Interviews in a Week*, we have been challenged by individuals and situations which have made us stop and think about the way interviews are conducted. We have continued to talk to people who have succeeded at interviews (some as a result of reading the book), and consulted colleagues who regularly interview. All this accumulated knowledge and experience is contained within this book.

By the end of the week you should feel better informed about the process – the content, style and motivations behind questions – as well as feeling more confident about presenting your experience, your knowledge, your skills and your abilities.

We would like you to think of this book as your companion and your guide through what can be uncharted waters. Your challenge is to apply this learning to yourself and the situations you face. Use the examples to develop a language and method of talking about yourself. This will lead to easy, flowing answers you can access even under pressure.

Remember that your interviewer is interested in you, not how you believe you should respond. Many interviewers are becoming wise to, and wary of, textbooks answers. So work on responses that will differentiate you from the other candidates and think about how to hold the interviewer's attention.

Sunday	What's involved?
Monday	Are you sitting comfortably?
Tuesday	Can you do the job?
Wednesday	Who are you?
Thursday	How will you do the job?
Friday	Will you fit?
Saturday	Are you ready?

By Saturday you will have a healthy portfolio of answers to produce at any interview. We hope you enjoy your week which provides everything you need to tackle the toughest of interviews successfully.

What's involved?

Today we will begin by summarising what's involved – what you are likely to encounter on your journey to the interview. We want to set the scene so that you are ready to concentrate on the questions that follow during the rest of the week.

What's involved?

- Objectives
- First steps
- Telephone screening
- Assessment centres
- What makes a question tough?

Objectives

Throughout the week you will have the opportunity to reflect on the reasoning behind the different kinds of questions you are asked. You will be able to consider your own aims. It is amazing how many interviewees expect the interviewer to be so in charge of the interview that they disempower themselves by not having their own clear plan and set of objectives. If you don't know specifically what you want from a job, how will you know when you achieve it?

Today's objectives relate to overall considerations of what's involved for both parties in the lead-in to the interview itself.

Interviewer's objectives	Interviewee's objectives
To get the right person for the job with:	*To find the job I want by:*
• key interpersonal skills	• creating a positive impression from the start
• relevant qualifications	• being prepared mentally and physically
• high energy	• getting to know the organisation
• a record of quality results	• anticipating questions
• initiative	• having something to say
	• feeling confident

It is vitally important that the interviewer selects the right person the first time, otherwise they might upset the balance of the team, have to look over their shoulder at a rival, or, at worst, have to suffer the expense in terms of time and cost of re-advertising and recruiting anew. Interviewers are also aware that the interview process itself is flawed so the process is often made up of different steps.

First steps

Good interviewers will have invested a significant amount of time in the planning process – scoping the role, allocating a budget, talking to the stakeholders, defining the competencies and the person specification, planning the advertisement and briefing headhunters or recruitment consultants. After receiving applications, the tasks are far from over. The interviewer, or someone else in the organisation, has to arrange the first steps:

- long listing
- short listing
- first interviews – sometimes telephone
- second interviews
- assessments
- meeting the stakeholders

Be aware that the more responsible the role, the more involved the key stakeholders will be. This may mean greater demands on your time because it may involve a series of meetings.

Telephone screening

The route to receiving an invitation to an interview can differ from organisation to organisation. Letters of application accompanied by CVs are the preferred way to present yourself and give information on your qualifications, experience and career to date. Increasingly this information is acceptable on-line. Your aim is to sell yourself in no more than two pages, giving the reader what they need to make their decision. There is help at hand from a book in this series, *CVs in a Week*. Some organisations use application forms, and the same applies to an application form as applies to a CV. Don't forget to sell yourself, even though your style may be cramped by the space available or questions asked – be creative.

Many organisations screen their long list of applicants by using a telephone interview. The purpose of the conversation is to create a realistic short list for the next stage. Only a small number of the candidates will progress beyond this stage so don't underestimate the importance of this conversation.

Often a screening interview will be unannounced: don't be put off by this. The interviewer normally asks whether it is convenient to talk so you can always buy some time and ring the person back. Your preparation is essential – you will need to think through what you say, how you say it and what you want the interviewer to remember. Also consider the limits of time; whilst we know of screening interviews that have lasted over an hour, it is more likely that you have under 20 minutes. Check whom exactly you are speaking to and don't make any assumptions.

Case history: One senior manager screening applicants for a key post in her team, rang an applicant to discuss certain aspects of his CV. He was unable to talk immediately. When she answered the phone, he assumed he was speaking to an administrative assistant and was both sharp and dismissive. Once he realised he was talking to his potential boss, his manner changed. But it was too late and there was no way he was going through to the next stage.

Pre-screening is one of the most challenging stages as making an impact with only your voice is extremely difficult. When you listen to an interview on the radio or have a telephone conversation, you probably only listen to a small amount of the conversation. Who do you listen to and why? What is it about their conversation that holds your attention? It's then up to you to build these techniques into your conversation with the interviewer! Use pace and tone to punctuate what you are saying. Think about what makes a voice attractive to you. Relax your jaw and mouth by repeating the sounds 'me – you' a number of times to help. If nothing else it will make you laugh which in turn will relieve any tension.

Be prepared – what you say

- Which parts of your CV to highlight
- Make it interesting
- Relate what you say to the role

Be prepared – how you say it

- Speak up and out
- Use tone and pace
- Be relaxed
- Smile

Some organisations are now using video conferencing for this screening and you are asked to attend an anonymous office with what looks like a computer screen. Don't be put off by the technology. Arrive early and become familiar with the surroundings. In global organisations this is as commonplace as a telephone link.

If you are one of those lucky people who receive headhunters calls on a regular basis, treat all these seriously. They may lead to the opportunity you are looking for.

Assessment Centres

Every organisation wants to make the best decision. The amount of investment in terms of time and money (advertising, head hunters/agency costs, etc.) can be immense. This, balanced by the fact that interviews are proven to be one of the least reliable methods of selection, means that you will probably experience more than just a traditional question and answer session. The word 'interview' can be used to include a multitude of experiences, including:

- Presentations
- Group exercises
- Tests – psychometric and ability tests
- In trays
- On-the-job assessments

All of these exercises are devised to give you an opportunity to shine rather than to trip you up. Find out which are going to be on the agenda for your interview and develop a strategy for managing them. It is likely you have had to make a presentation, contribute to a group discussion, manage your in-tray or be assessed via performance reviews. As these are nothing new, merely a different environment, you can be prepared for the unexpected. Remember that you have plenty of knowledge and experience to manage it well.

What often happens when individuals are asked to prepare for a presentation is that it becomes the only thing they focus on and they produce a wonderfully slick presentation, but everything else suffers. Whatever you are informed of in advance, it is worth preparing yourself for more and even contacting the named person to find out more about the process.

Tests fall into a number of categories:

- verbal

- numerical

- skill

- spatial

- personality/psychometric.

Skilled assessors should only choose tests which have a relevance to the role. You may be asked to complete some tests at home, others will take place in a classroom environment and be timed. If you haven't sat any tests before, there are books and people who can help you including *Psychometric Testing in a week*. Most parts of the process have an equal weighting, so overlooking any part in your preparation will affect your overall performance. For more information on Assessment Centres, see *Assessment Centres in a week*.

What makes a question tough?

The concept of a tough question is usually a matter of personal interpretation. Sometimes an interviewer will deliberately ask what they consider to be a tough question; on other occasions they may hit your Achilles' heel without intent.

You may already have a clear idea of your 'tricky' areas. If so, it is a good idea to think about them now instead of hoping they might be missed. Compile a table like the one below to help you.

What constitutes a tough question?	Why?	How will I combat this?
Gaps in employment	....	....
Industry/technical knowledge	....	....
Health problems	....	....
Why I am leaving	....	....

If the question is tough because it is a surprise either in content or timing, take a deep breath, and think about what you have been asked. You can't prepare for the content of a surprise question, but you can prepare a general response. Practise the skill of checking with the interviewer that you have understood what has just been asked without simply echoing their question. *'Let me be clear – you are asking me . . . So you want to know how precisely I would . . .'* This is a useful technique if the question requires you to go to a level of explanation that feels uncomfortable to you. This buys you some thinking time, too. Watch politicians, they are expert at this technique.

Why do interviewers ask 'tough' questions? In many cases they want to gain a deeper understanding in a particular area – either a greater insight of you or to check the extent of your knowledge and expertise. They may need to test your response to the types of pressure demanded by the job.

The way to answer tough questions is to be confident that if you have done your preparation you will have a reasonable answer somewhere in your repertoire. Go for that rather than struggling to find a 'perfect' answer; just like the 'perfect' question they don't exist! While every question the interviewer asks has a purpose, it is unwise to answer until you know:

- the reason for the question
- the most appropriate answer
- how to reply positively

Over the next few days, notice whether your automatic responses to any questions tend to be framed in positive or negative language. When you use negative words like 'trouble', 'problem' and 'disaster', you base your thinking in a negative framework.

The interviewer will join you there and be in a negative set too. If you use language in a positive vein, then you will feel more confident and can expect the interviewer to respond in a more friendly and co-operative manner. Use words like 'opportunity', 'challenge' and 'learning'. Consider the different impacts and choose to be more positive.

Summary

Today we have considered interviews and their part in the recruitment process. Whilst the other tools that organisations use are either organisation or role specific, the preparation you do for interview is essential to your success. Here are some simple rules to help you.

- Stay calm
- Listen to the question
- Speak clearly and steadily
- Tell the truth
- Avoid talking too much
- Make it relevant

You need to understand the interviewer, and by simply listening and reflecting back the language and pace of the interviewer you can demonstrate this understanding. Before you jump in with your response you need to think about the question, considering why it has been asked and what the interviewer wants to find out. If you understand this, then you are able to answer the question comprehensively, presenting yourself well and leaving the interviewer with no need to ask you any supplementary questions.

By doing your research well, you should also have picked up some of the language from company reports, or any information you are given about the job, department and organisation. If you would like further information on how to conduct this research, we devote a day (Monday) to research in the companion to this book, *Succeeding at Interviews in a Week*.

Tomorrow we will ensure that you are ready to make a positive first impression.

Are you sitting comfortably?

You've passed the first stage of the recruitment process – well done! Your application and responses suggest that you could do the job and fit in. You've successfully answered the screening questions or passed the tests giving the right mix of content and style to help with the decision making process. Your task now is to influence the interviewer from thinking you 'could' do the job, to thinking you 'can' and 'will' do it successfully. Whatever the next stage, it is important that you feel comfortable enough to succeed by:

- Presenting yourself well
- Meeting and greeting with ease
- Establishing relationships
- Opening moves

If you have done your homework and prepared yourself well, you will be setting yourself up for success right from the start. Even before you meet the person who is going to interview you, you will be party to a mutual weighing up. The opening stages of the interview can be very influential, as both you and the interviewer want to impress each other.

Interviewer's objectives	Interviewee's objectives
• Did they impress all the people they met?	• Do I create a good impression?
• Do they look the part?	• Can I do myself justice?
• Will they settle in quickly?	• Does the place feel and look good?
• Can they be easily understood?	• Did they make me feel 'at home'?

SO PLEASED TO MEET YOU

The letter arrives or you receive a call inviting you to the interview. The first thing that comes into your head is normally a good indicator of how you feel about interviews – some people love the opportunity to talk about themselves; the thought of the experience is positive and the outcome excites them.

Other people dread interviews, they hate the predictability of the questions they will be asked; they feel more competent than most of the interviewers they are faced with; they don't like having to sell themselves; they believe their achievements should suffice.

Positive thinking	**Negative thinking**
• My application must have made an impression . . . • I've got through the first stage . . .	• Oh no! • Do I really want the job . . .? • Can I be bothered to go through this routine again . . .

- I'm obviously what they're looking for . . .
- All I need to do is impress the interviewer . . .
- What will I face . . .?
- What exactly will they be looking for . . .?
- Can I do the job . . .?

You should begin by thinking positively if you are a person who tends to dread the interview process; your personal preparation should start immediately. If you have to ring to confirm your appointment, make sure you have some prompts, which may include what you want to clarify. Take a deep breath and start by smiling. Your voice will give away how you feel about the process.

You may have been invited to attend an informal interview. Beware, there is no such thing as an informal interview, and every meeting should be treated with careful thought and consideration.

Presenting yourself well

Arriving
You will have checked the date, time and place of the interview and have arrived with time to spare. You should use this time to take in the surroundings. Relax, stand tall, breathe deeply and remember how you want to present yourself.

Entering the bulding
When you enter the building, take the opportunity to chat to the receptionist. Be natural, but don't present yourself as trying too hard to make a good impression, although it is one of your aims. The opinions of people at security entrances

and receptions, in fact any staff you might encounter, are often considered

> *Case history* – Generally my receptionist will see candidates first. I look carefully at their reaction to her – whether they treat her with respect and friendliness or disdain and condescension. I always ask her what she thinks overall and how she thinks they would fit into our department. It all affects my decisions.

This cuts both ways. You will also have intuitive responses to the first people you meet, so attend to those responses. Would you want to be represented by such people and could you work in those conditions? The overall efficiency and genuine customer service with which you are treated may impress you. On the other hand you may be disappointed by being kept waiting or by the lack of organisation – it may be a bad day rather than an indicator of their style.

Remember that for whoever you deal with from the start, you will be just one of their tasks for the day. As far as you are concerned, of course, you are the only person going for the interview.

How you present yourself counts. Make good eye contact, look around you and take notice of what you see and hear. These all give you a feel for the organisation. There may be company literature to read, which can give you further insight, or even the basis for a question in the interview. They may offer you a drink, and it's fine to accept it, but you may have other things to do:

- visit the toilet
- check how you look
- look through your file
- read your answers to questions
- prepare your responses
- relax

First impressions
First impressions are important, so how you sit, how you make eye contact with whoever approaches you, the quality of your handshake and how you look will al make an impact. Interviewers will notice uncleaned shoes, dirty fingernails, style and mannerisms. For most jobs, the impressions we make on our colleagues, clients and managers matter. How you look at the interview will be taken to indicate how you would look and conduct yourself when working.

You can anticipate their first words and prepare your responses accordingly. That way you can avoid blurting out something nonsensical such as 'Goodnight' or 'Sorry'. If you know that you suffer from either verbal diarrhoea or paralysis when you're nervous, a few practised responses will stand you in good stead. Only continue your conversation with the receptionist or secretary if you get a favourable response. If the reception is busy, then the replies will be limited and you need to show your awareness of this.

Your first challenge is to introduce yourself and make polite and interesting conversation before you even start the interview. Make sure you have thought about your opening remarks in advance. If you have a number of comments ready at the beginning, their familiarity will calm you down. The earlier you can say your name, the better. It's something you know very well and because you don't have to think about it, you will be able to start with your 'normal' voice rather than a nervous, high pitched squeak.

Your first words

- Hello, I'm . . . I've come for an interview with . . .
- What's the agenda for the day?
- How do most people travel into work?
- What a fascinating building. How long have you been based here?
- How does it compare with your offices at . . .?
- Do you have any company brochures I can read while I'm waiting?

Meeting and greeting with ease
When you enter the room, the interview is ready to begin – well nearly. Sitting down and getting comfortable are important. It is likely that the room has been set out for an interview, but sometimes you will be interviewed from behind a desk. If you are not directed to a chair, it is appropriate to say, when invited to sit down. *Will this be OK?*

Be careful not to sit in direct sunlight otherwise your squint or frown caused by the bright light may be misinterpreted as your normal expression. You may be asked if you want a drink. Do remember that juggling with a drink when you are talking may be difficult. Asking for water is the safest option, particularly as you can expect to be doing most of the talking for up to an hour.

If there is more than one interviewer, you should, at this stage, be introduced to all of them. A simple: *Yes, we've spoken*, or *Pleased to meet you*, gives you the chance to talk and keep your voice loosened. The interviewer may then describe the interview process, where this stage fits and what comes next. They may also describe the role you've applied for in the context of the organisation. You may be asked at the end of this section whether everything is clear. A brief *Yes, thanks*, is all that's needed to signal that you're both ready to start. If you're unclear, ask for clarification.

The interviewer may then go through some of the same questions you have already been asked, so you will be well practised at answering these: *How was your journey? Did you get here Ok?*

These questions are simply breaking the ice, so be careful not to go into a long monologue about transport, and resist the temptation to say the obvious or be sarcastic. This is not an opportunity to talk about the amount of traffic on the roads, how you hate commuting or the state of the public transport system. Your answers should be short but warm. If any conversation is to develop from this, make it positive. *Fine. The roads were clear and your map was a great help. I enjoy my travel time as it gives me time to plan.*

How long did it take you?
If this is the office base you will be working from, they will be interested in your commute. Research shows that because of the uncertainty surrounding employment, more people are establishing a base and travelling to wherever there work is. Some families now have more than one home to help them manage their commute. Most organisations, however, prefer that their employees live within a certain radius of their place of work and some even stipulate it. This question, whilst simple on the surface, may have an underlying query about your flexibility: *The train only took 35 minutes and I took advantage of that time.*

Establishing relationships

At this point your intention is to relax and keep your voice active and loosened up. As well as settling yourself down, you want to get into the rhythm of the person with whom you are speaking. Research suggests that people tend to like people who are like them. If you make the effort to be like someone else, they will feel more comfortable in their dealings with you. (On Friday we will consider how this relates to the question, Will you fit?)

Notice the pace at which the interviewer speaks, and try to speed up or slow down to match. Once you are synchronised, you may be able to lead them to a pace that better suits you.

Opening moves

What follows are a range of questions to warm you up, get you talking, giving both of you time to settle into the interview. Some of the toughest questions are those that give you enormous scope, such as:

- Talk me through your career to date
- What are the highlights of your career?
- Take me through your CV/résumé

Most readers will have experienced questions such as these. They are used early in the interview to see how you cope and whether you are able to give a lucid and relevant response. Your interviewer wants to know how you present yourself in relation to your career. Your answer to these questions should give them clues to your suitability and the areas they may want to expand later on.

Don't panic when you hear these questions. You should be well prepared, in control and able to respond effectively. In preparing for the interview you will have thought about your personality and strengths, picking out the qualities which show that you are well matched to the organisation and job, thus allowing you to describe how you are the ideal employee to be recruited.

You may choose to ask them: *Is there a particular part of my background that interests you?* Be aware of questions in response to questions, as they often do not give you the answers you want. They may respond by: *The parts which equip you for this role!* The question, *Whould you prefer a chronological or skills-based review?* may elicit the response: *Whichever will give us the best overview of you.*

One other cautionary note is that this is a warm-up question; it is not intended to take the whole of the interview. Do not focus on every role, project and conversation you have had. The interviewer is still settling down and giving you something you can easily talk about to get the interview going.

Choose what you say carefully – your description of your career should be entertaining and no longer than four minutes. You may decide to start by saying:

I see the start of my career as when I had to make choices at school and university as these have influenced all my future experiences.

I was clear what I wanted to do from an early stage and have followed that through a, b, c, whilst developing my skills . . ., to the point that I reach today. I am now seeking an opportunity to stretch and develop myself further.

There are two significant themes in my career – my skills and the environments in which I have worked. I have developed my skills which are . . . and my success has depended on them. The environments in which I have applied them are diverse . . . I enjoy working in different environments.

I started my career at . . . as I was seeking to . . . I then sought to develop both my skills and knowledge by moving companies and chose to join . . . because of their reputation for . . . This has been the pattern throughout my career.

Whatever you say, you should demonstrate or refer to one or more of your key behavioural attributes. Your interviewers will want to know what you have done in addition to how you have done it. It will help them if you can look back to describe past achievements and then project forward to say how they will apply and benefit this post.

You may, depending on the context, want to refer to:

- improvements
- turnover
- people managed
- projects completed
- savings instigated
- budgets managed

This is a time for you to shine, so don't discuss problems you had with previous employers or managers. Take some time to think about yourself. These questions are not easy to answer off the cuff, but you can prepare for them.

Once you have safely navigated your way around these early questions you can be confident and ready to concentrate on the more weighty ones that will undoubtedly follow.

Summary

Remember, in the opening stages:

- Start well
- Everyone you meet may be asked for an opinion
- There is no such thing as an informal interview
- Be relaxed
- Sit comfortably
- Use your warm up questions to your advantage

Tomorrow we will focus on the questions surrounding *What have you done so far?* This will help the interviewer to understand that you can do the job!

What have you done so far?

The introductions are over. You are in the interview room. Your interviewer has talked you through the role, the organisation and what to expect. You sense that the interview for real is about to begin.

Interviewer's objectives	Interviewee's objectives
	To demonstrate that:
• Can you do the job?	• I could do the job given the opportunity
• Do you have the skills and experience?	• I have what you need
• Do you match your CV?	• I am articulate
• Are you qualified?	• My achievements speak for themselves
• Do you match our competencies?	• I could add value

Today we will focus on the following areas:

- work history and experience
- training and qualifications
- competence.

Normally this phase of the interview is not populated by the toughest questions. The interviewer is wanting factual answers, but don't waste an opportunity – tell your interviewers not just what your goals were, but how you achieved them, and what this has taught you for the future.

Work history and experience

Your jobs, projects, experience, achievements and career
choices are of interest to the interviewer at this stage.
Do you have what they need to do the job? They will ask:

- What have you done?
- What have you achieved?
- In what ways have you achieved your goals?
- Why did you leave?

What have you done?

Your response to questions in this section should recognise
the interviewer's motivation for asking them. They are not
wanting a regurgitation of your job titles or organisations;
they want to go below the surface to hear about how you
have contributed to the success of the team, department,

company or group. Their questions may reflect this, but even if they don't, your answers should!

Talke me through your career to date?
This question is asked for a variety of reasons. As we mentioned yesterday, it can be used as a warm up, or it can be used to reacquaint them with your CV. Your interviewer should already have read through your CV so in this question they want a 'whistle-stop' tour of what you've done. We emphasise the whistle-stop, so be succinct and precise! Make sure your words match what you have put on paper, and beware of too much detail such as dates, who you reported to, responsibilities.

My career has spanned four different organisations and has been about acquiring knowledge and skills and applying these to each different role. Each role has contributed to the person I am today and supports the contribution I can make to your company.

Your interviewer may as the question, *What brings you here?* in a variety of different ways. This question indicates your interviewer is interested in the choices you have made in your career, and how your skills have developed through your different roles and organisations. You have to be selective in your answers and choose the elements that demonstrate individual and organisation benefits.

I have enjoyed a successful and varied career. My first job gave me an opportunity to develop my people management and leadership skills. I managed a team of 40 on three different sites, establishing set procedures and monitoring the service level. I then moved on to develop more specialist skills in a sister organisation, managing projects and achieving the deadlines set, always coming in under budget and always on target. I am now seeking an opportunity in

*which I can bring together both these sets of skills and develop
them.*

Tell me about your responsibilities in your present job?
This is not an opportunity to recite the twenty responsibilities
outlined in your job description or your competencies. It's an
opportunity to blow your own trumpet. Wherever possible,
summarise your responsibilities. The more you can describe
them in terms of the benefits they bring to the organisation,
the better.

*I have four main responsibilities . . . Balancing these and setting
targets to ensure my team achieves them has been a challenge,
particularly in a climate of managing a reduced cost base. I have
been successful and my success in the role has been due to my
ability to manage and control the work of the team.*

What have you achieved?

This style of question is relatively easy to respond to, if you
have prepared.

How is your effectiveness in your present post measured?
Measures are important to most organisations. Even if your
role isn't formally measured you should think about how
you quantify your success. It gives the interviewer some
ideas of the scope of your role, what you have achieved and
the potential contribution you could make to their
organisation.

*The principal measure is the business review process. I have both a
cost and a revenue budget for which I am fully accountable. The
bottom line is what counts most. Apart from this, I have the*

freedom to make decisions. I enjoy being measured as I can always focus my attention on identifying and working towards improvements.

2005   2000   1995

Tell me about a recent project. What aspects of it gave you the most satisfaction?

Pick a good example. Don't just go for personal satisfaction, although that is the essence of the question. Also focus on the immediate- and long-term benefits.

They asked me to reorganise a department. I did my research, reading and talking to the key stakeholders. I identified four key improvements which could save over £10,000 a year and implemented them over the next two months.

Have you done the best work you are capable of?
Say 'yes' and the interviewer will think you're a 'has been'.
Your focus on this question should be on how you could
apply and develop your skills further.

*I'm proud of my work achievements to date. But I believe the best is
yet to come. I'm always motivated to give my best efforts and in
this job there are always opportunities to contribute and improve.*

*In what ways has your job prepared you to take on greater
responsibility?*
The interviewer is looking for examples of professional
development, perhaps to judge your future growth potential,
so you must tell a story that demonstrates this.

*When I first started, my boss would brief me daily. I made mistakes,
learnt a lot and met all my deadlines. As time went by I took on
greater responsibilities. Now I meet with her weekly to discuss any
strategic changes so that she can keep management informed. I
think that demonstrates not only my growth but also the confidence
my manager has in my judgement and ability to perform
consistently above standard.*

In what ways have you achieved your goals?

What has made you successful in your current position?
Here the interviewer is trying to find out not just what, but
how. You may want to talk about your influencing skills,
your persistence, your understanding of the business needs,
timing or whatever else has made you successful.

*I believe my success is due to my ability to recognise who it is I
need to get on my side. I then start to influence them by identifying
the business benefits and get them to sponsor the project at the*

highest level. I keep these people constantly updated on progress, giving them an opportunity to continue to contribute by challenging the blocks I experience.

What problems have you met in relationships with your present colleagues and what techniques have you developed to overcome them?

We only achieve things in organisations through other people, but often we do experience blocks of some kind. This doesn't mean that the interviewer expects problems with the role or your relationships; it means they are trying to uncover what strategies you have for dealing with disappointments, blocks, obstacles or the culture of the organisation in which you have worked. You should be honest and positive about how you have tackled these; you may want to include a bit about your learning.

My role was about change and I knew there would be resistance. The resistance I experienced was subtle – it involved only giving me a part of the story, not following through on actions and undermining me with colleagues. The best technique I found for dealing with this was by recording on paper all key conversations where decisions were made, giving timescales for action. I would then distribute them to all the other key stakeholders. It seemed to work. My colleagues understood that I would not lie down and accept their behaviour and they changed. This isn't my preferred style but I adapted my style to the people and the situation.

What are the most difficult decisions you have made in the last six months? What made them difficult?

Your interviewer is interested in what you find difficult and wherever possible you should balance this with a strength. You may want to talk about managing people, or others' expectations or that you have stretch goals and this challenges you in terms of prioritising.

Due to the cost of savings which had to be achieved, I needed to make a member of my team redundant. It was a very tough decision as she made a valuable contribution to the team, but I just needed to find a more cost-effective way to deliver. My biggest challenge was to communicate this to her in a way she understood and was not too damaging. I think I achieved this through careful planning and preparation.

How do you feel about your progress to date?
This question is not only about your progress but also asks you to rate your self-esteem. Be positive. Help the interviewer believe you see each day as an opportunity to learn and contribute. That you see their organisation's environment being conducive to your best efforts.

In looking back over my career I am very pleased about my progress, I have achieved all that I have set myself and more. I have identified opportunities that would stretch and develop me and been pleased with my achievements. I am now seeking to maintain this momentum.

Why did you leave?

Questions on the decisions you made that prompted you to seek a change in your role or organisation should be answered with a degree of caution. Many people, when answering these questions fall into the trap of focusing on what wasn't right rather than what was. Focus on the 'pulls' (what drove you forward) rather than the 'pushes' (what made you want to leave).

Pull factors

- Seeking fresh challenge
- New organisation/products
- Working with new people
- Belief in vision

Push factors

- Boredom
- Relationship with boss
- Asked to resign
- Redundancy

ADMIN   R+D

What made you leave – after 10 years with them?
Here the underlying question is 'what went wrong?'
Organisations are now looking for a mixture of loyalty and
exposure to different environments, cultures, projects and
people. In answering this question you have to walk the fine
line between demonstrating this loyalty and commitment
whilst seeking fresh challenges and being flexible and
adaptable. Make sure that you also pace whatever moves you

have made within a context of a long term strategy, even if it didn't feel that at the time – every move should be seen as moving towards a career goal.

I wanted a position that would give me more responsibility, a position in which I could put into practice what I had been learning. I recognised that this wasn't available to me at . . .

What do you want from your next job that isn't in your current position?
This question has a slight twist in its tail. It should always be answered positively and be tailored to the position you are applying for.

An opportunity to apply my . . . skills in a new team, with a different set of customers and in a different environment. The challenge will come from all those changes. I know I can make a contribution and from what you've been describing, it sounds even more exciting.

Why have you applied for this job?
This is one question you should expect, if it doesn't come in this form, it may be couched in *why* . . . (the organisation)? You need to be sure of 'why' as it will be obvious from your body language if you are not convinced, committed or clear. Your reasons may be opportunity, challenge, and association.

From all I know about the role, it is exactly what I am looking for. My knowledge of your organization from talking to employees and reading the literature you sent, tells me it is somewhere I would fit in particularly well.

Case history – One candidate when asked why he wanted to be an accountant, responded, 'Well, I don't really, but I've been told it's a good profession and it pays well. I think you're a good company to work for'. He didn't get the job!

Training and qualifications

Interviewers tend not to make assumptions on the basis of people's qualifications because they are more interested in people's competence. Competence relates to the skills, knowledge and behaviours which, combined, produce the required results. This generally reflects a shift from the concept of education to the concept of learning: from input (classroom-based learning) to outputs (self-paced learning, coaching); from becoming qualified to continuous professional development. You will probably be asked less about the institutions or courses you've attended, and more about how you have applied your learning.

What have you done since you first qualified to keep your knowledge up to date?
The interviewer is keen to understand how you are continually updating yourself to the external environment. You can demonstrate this in a range of ways – books, coaching, shadowing, conferences, project groups, training courses, professional associations, journals, the Internet. Make sure you give a balanced response. Present yourself as someone who has taken responsibility for their own development and seeks regular opportunities to learn.

I read journals and papers. I attend workshops through the Institute. I seek opportunities to work alongside people I feel I can learn from and attend courses and conferences.

Which of your qualifications do you see as relevant to this post, and how?
In answering this question you need to think carefully about what skills this role requires. If it's a technical role, then you should refer to your technical qualifications and experience. If it's more a management role, then refer to whatever training or qualifications you have. Do not be put off if you don't have formal qualifications. Talk through your learning.

My degree, whilst some time ago, has given me a good grounding in the principles, models and practice of . . . Whilst I have studied for my Masters and a Diploma in Management Studies, the qualifications most relevant to the role are not so much of the accredited type, but more to do with 10 years of success in the role with achievements both personal and professional.

Whtat important changes are taking place in your field? Do you consider them to be good or bad?
This question tests how up to date you are, so you may want to clarify it in terms of your function or sector. They are also asking for your opinion, which is a little more tricky; all you can do is be honest. Your interviewer is not wanting someone who sits on the fence, but if there are good and bad points you should state them. Think about what 'good' and 'bad' means to you, and what they might mean to the interviewer.

Competence

As we mentioned previously, competencies are now commonplace in most organisations. They don't simply focus on *what* you do, but *how* you do it.

Competencies make the interview process much more focused and less dependent on the intuition and gut reaction of the interviewer. The competencies for the role are normally available to applicants. If you haven't received these then do request them as they are an essential part of your preparation. By reading them, you will get an idea of the culture and what is important to the organisation. You can then frame your answers to reflect this.

Competencies may also include characteristics such as resilience and influence. The questions you may be asked in order to uncover these areas of competence may be:

Resilience

- How do you bounce back after a setback?
- How would I know you were under pressure?
- In what ways has your boss disappointed you?
- What does resilience mean to you?
- When have you demonstrated resilience?

Relate your answers to your own experience and related aspects of your work, not how you recovered after having a puncture on the way to an airport.

Influencing

- Describe a time when you got the solution you wanted?
- Whose support have you found elusive and why?
- How do you influence others?
- Tell me when you persuaded someone senior to do something they were unwilling to do.
- How would I know you were trying to change my mind? I have a preferred candidate for this role – change my mind.
- Which areas of influence challenge you most?

Summary

Today, we have concentrated on the questions concerned with: *Can you do the job?* Think about what you've done and how you've applied your learning:

- Sell yourself
- Make sure your words complement what you have said on paper
- Present your career in a logical, planned and progressive manner
- Convince the interviewer that you can do the job
- Present your learning in terms of competence, not solely formal qualifications
- Use transferable skills

These questions offer you an opportunity to sell yourself to the organisation. Be focused and clear, and sell yourself as just the person they are seeking. Tomorrow we will begin to help you understand how best to answer more personal questions.

Who are you?

You should now be confident about describing what you have done in your career, and be able to talk convincingly about your experience, skills, competence and qualifications. Today considers who you are in terms of:

- Self assessment
- Personality
- Achievements
- Strengths and weaknesses
- Perceptions
- Leisure

Interviewers want you to bring to life the person you presented in your CV or application letter. Depending on the type of job, they will need to know if you are a team player or a loner, a concrete thinker or an ideas person.

They will be constantly asking themselves – is this the kind of person we need for the post?

Interviewer's objectives	Interviewee's objectives
• Are you easy to get to know? • Can you talk about yourself? • Does your personality fit?	• Be honest and open • Be able to describe myself succinctly • Portray my personality accurately

We would encourage you to give an assessment of yourself which shows a confident and informed individual. Dependent on the post, this is also the chance to describe your life outside the job. Be intuitive: put yourself in the interviewer's shoes. You want the interviewer to feel that you can get along with them and their organisation. This is your opportunity to make the most of yourself. The skill is to get the balance right. The way you talk about yourself and your work; your team's and your organisation's achievements, your work and leisure.

Self assessment

Self knowledge is increasingly important in the world of work. You are expected to know yourself – your skills, characteristics and limitations. You are expected to understand what impact these may have on your performance and, of course, be seeking to develop and improve. The interviewer will be interested in how you manage self-assessment questions. For your part you need to think about the *you* you want to present. Some people find all the questions that ask them to describe themselves *tough*. If this is you, it is well worth spending some time analysing your anxiety and working out ways to combat it. The key to overcoming anxiety is planning and practice, so think about your responses in advance and practise saying them out loud.

Anxiety	Solution
Once I start talking, I won't know when to stop.	Write the main points and time yourself as you say them – aim for no more than 2 minutes.
I've nothing to say about myself.	Complete the sentence 'I am . . .' at least 50 times and then assess your responses.
How can I know what they want?	Go back to your earlier research and note the type of person you would be looking for to fill the post. Pick out what relates to you.
They will think I am being arrogant.	They want you to be confident about yourself and aware of who you are. Select truthful evidence.

It is certain that these kinds of questions will emerge at some stage during the interview, so overcome your anxiety if it exists. Be proud of who you are, and what you have achieved, and present it in a way that convinces the interviewer. Use every source of information to inform your preparation. Ask colleagues for feedback, look over the comments from your appraisals, think about projects you were particularly proud of or enjoyed. If you have completed tests, these may help. All these sources say something about who you are. Also think about examples to back up statements, as your interviewers will be interested in how you present the evidence. Self-assessment questions come in a variety of forms, the most common ones are:

- Tell me about yourself?
- How would you describe yourself?
- What are you like as a person?
- How would your colleagues describe you?

It is worth experimenting with different statements to describe who you are. Take a couple of sentences from your 'I am' list and play around with them: *I am an ideas person . . . I am easy going . . . I am in charge of the catering outlet . . . I enjoy challenges . . .*

Now start to flesh out your statements with examples that demonstrate how they relate to the job and the organisation. Create a sense of your value to the potential employer and the benefits you can offer. Prepare a statement that is powerful, accurate and that demonstrates what differentiates you from other candidates:

I am creative and identify unconventional ways of tackling a situation. At . . ., I often put forward suggestions that saved the company time and money, whilst preserving the company image.

Answers to these questions will flow with practice. The skill is to make them relevant to your role and your interviewer.

Personality

You may be asked some questions that relate to specific personality types and traits which are considered necessary for the post. For example, if you are applying to manage a remote location, you will need to have a degree of independence; for a customer relations post, you will need to demonstrate tolerance and patience. Consider how the personality traits on the next page apply to you and the jobs you want.

However you describe your personality, be sure to have substantive examples and, wherever possible, give times and benefits:

I pride myself on my ability to act on my own initiative. We were keen to take on a project to assess waste management. There was no spare money to do this so I spoke to various local organisations to arrange a sponsorship programme.

Personality traits

Independence	Making decisions without supervision or reference
Patience	Calm and prepared to wait for the right time and place
Integrity	Takes responsibility for own actions, good and poor
Judgement	Evaluates data and courses of action rationally
Adaptability	Responds effectively to change
Compliance	Adheres to company policy/procedures
Tenacity	Demonstrates staying power in challenging situations
Commitment	Belief in job/role and its value to the company
Decisive	Readiness to take actions and make decisions
Dependability	Staying power and stamina
Confidence	Calmly aware and comfortable with who you are

Here are some other questions to think through.

What are your likes?
This is a rather vague question, but it may be chosen in contrast to what you are like as a person to see how you respond.

I like challenges. I always set personal goals to try and push myself that bit further and to feel I've achieved something.

What are your dislikes?
This inevitably follows 'what are your likes'. The interviewer may be wanting to know how compatible your personal values are with the role.

Be wary of criticising your former boss and colleagues, or implying that you were unhappy about working hard, doing boring tasks or dealing with the less pleasant aspects of your work. Also steer clear of launching into a tirade about dislikes of pot noodles and other trivia.

I try to be honest and act with integrity. I dislike it when others lie, blame or don't show the same commitment to the task or the company as I do.

How have you benefited from your disappointments?
Disappointments are different from failures. It is an intelligent interviewer who asks this question. The question itself is very positive – it enables you to talk about what you have learnt from your setbacks and how it has changed your approach.

I treat disappointments as learning: I look at what has happened, why it happened and how I would do things differently at each stage should I face the same situation again.

Be yourself when you are answering these questions. After all, it's not just what you say, it's the way that you say it. Part of your personality will shine through as you utter your response. Notice whether your body language complements or refutes your descriptions. It is no good suggesting that patience is one of your qualities if your foot is tapping in anticipation of the next question or, when talking about your energy and enthusiasm, you talk into your chest with a sullen expression.

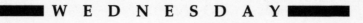

Strengths and limitations

It is well recognised that people have both strengths and
limitations. There will be parts of your personality that
support you and other parts that trip you up. Interviewers
ask about strengths and limitations as another way of
assessing your knowledge of yourself, your honesty and
your objectivity. They may also talk about weaknesses, areas
for improvement or personal development.

Before the interview you should spend some time thinking
about the characteristics that you make successful in
everything you undertake. What has contributed to making
you who you are today? It helps enormously if you can
portray a sense of self worth and confidence in what you do
well. If you can excite the interviewer with your enthusiasm,
they will assume you can do the same with their internal and
external customers.

I pride myself on being able to build rapport quickly with new people. In fact at . . . I was often asked to take visitors around the plant because the MD knew I would make them feel welcome and important.

Think through examples of your strengths balanced against the expectations for the job. For example, a manager might be expected to have strengths in planning, delegating, budgeting, time management, influencing people and managing relationships.

The interviewer will also expect you to give examples of how you are working to improve your limitations. Think about how you might have held yourself back in your career and your achievements. What has led you to feel frustrated and unhappy at work? You may come across some familiar areas for development that you can usefully admit to in an interview. Do remember that limitations can simply be the reverse side of a strength:

My eye for detail can be a great strength in designing copy, but a limitation when I'm managing people as I need to be convinced that everything is as it should be.

You have choices in presenting your limitations – you could focus on those strictly related to the post:
I am not familiar with the software you use. I became proficient with our present scheme in about 3 weeks and I'm sure I could do so with yours.

Or you can relate to your personality:
I am very particular about the way work goes out to clients. In my last appraisal we discussed the way this sometimes slows down output. We also agreed that without such attention to detail our

consistency and accuracy could be affected. I am working on finding a more balanced approach.

Some questions refer indirectly to strengths and limitations:

- Tell me about the last time you didn't delegate work to a subordinate and you were left handling a disproportionate amount of the workload?
- How did you feel about it?
- How did you handle the situation differently next time?

What are the most difficult situations you've faced?
How do you define 'difficult'? You must have a story ready for this one in which the situation was both tough and flexible enough to allow you to show yourself in a good light. Avoid talking about matters to do with other people. You can talk about a difficult decision to fire someone, but emphasise that once you had examined the problem and reached a conclusion you acted quickly and professionally, with the best interests of the company at heart.

What do you not have that we need for this post?
This is an easy response.
I think my skills match your requirements. I need more detailed product knowledge and experience of the company procedure.

Achievements

Achievements should be easy to identify. There is always something in our careers or lives that we feel particularly proud of: a project completed on time and budget against all odds; a crisis averted, people you managed, a bid that you won, a person you influenced. In fact, anything that had a happy ending. You should judge the merits of sticking to job-related accomplishments or whether it is appropriate to expand into your life outside the workplace.

I was proud to be part of the team that successfully guided the company towards a quality award.

I raised £ . . . for charity running in the London Marathon. I also picked up some business from my fellow runners along the way.

What has been your most creative achievement at work?

Although I feel my biggest achievements are still ahead of me, I am proud of my involvement in . . . with . . . I made my contribution as part of that team and learned a lot in the process. We succeeded through hard work, concentration and an eye for the bottom line.

What makes you stand out from the crowd?
A simple question, but it requires some thought. You can answer it in terms of increased revenues, decreased

operational costs, streamlined work flow. You may also want to think in terms of your characteristics.

I have a great track record for assuming responsibilities above and beyond the call of duty and I'm always willing to go the extra mile to get the job done well.

This reveals focus, direction, a sense of strength and determination. There are many different styles of 'achievement' questions: *Tell me about some of the toughest groups that you have had to get co-operation from. Did you have any formal authority? What did you do?*

Perceptions

Once you have given an account of your ideas about yourself, you are likely to be asked what other people think of you. Take care not to be flippant or to regurgitate what you have already said. Also be mindful that some of the people mentioned may have written, or be about to write, your references. It is important to be consistent. Ideally it would be good to check with your referees what they might write. Where that is not possible try to recall conversations and appraisal discussions you have had with them. You may be asked a selection of the following questions:

- How might your current colleagues describe you?
- What would your boss tell me about you?
- What is likely to be in your references?
- How would your staff describe you?
- How might one of your closest friends describe you?
- How might your worst enemy describe your character?

In my last appraisal my manager said how much he appreciated my candidness. He knows that I think very carefully before giving feedback and then do so in a professional way.

My staff know that I represent them positively in any organisational issues that may concern them. I know from feedback at appraisals that they trust me to keep their interests at the top of my agenda.

We can never underestimate the power of perceptions. Remember our comments from Monday that the perception people have of you will count. Anxiety can create the wrong impression, so by managing your anxiety you should be better able to manage perceptions.

Leisure

Leisure is a very important part of who you are. Because of the nature of the commitment that work now demands, interviewers are wanting to hear about the balance you strive for, to preserve your energy, or simply recuperate and switch off from the challenges of the day. It also gives the interviewer a fuller picture of who you are outside work. The following questions are a selection of those you may be asked:

- If you were on a desert island, what book would you take and why?
- What was the last book you read/film you saw and how did it affect you?
- How do you relax?
- What do you do for your holidays?
- What do you do in the evenings and weekends?

Be prepared for these questions. It makes sense to decide before the interview whether there is a particular film or book you want to mention because it says something about you that you want to convey.

Do you escape into thrillers and spy stories, or immerse yourself in science fiction? You may be a fan of the classics or poetry, romance, politics or sport.

Many people enjoy personal development books or tapes – there are no right or wrong answers, and these are not trick questions. Having said that, it is crucial that you have read or seen whatever you discuss so that you can talk about it with knowledge and enthusiasm.

> *Case history:* We spoke to one candidate who, at interview, enthused about *Pride and Prejudice* and was asked if they had read *Middlemarch*. They replied honestly, 'no', and were relieved when the interviewer suggested that it was a book they thought the candidate would thoroughly enjoy. Imagine the embarrassment if they had said 'yes', and then been expected to discuss it.

How do you wind down after a busy and pressured time at work? With increasing awareness of the long-term effects of stress, enlightened employers are recognising the importance of recovery time for their staff. It is important to demonstrate that you know how to look after yourself and keep yourself mentally and physically agile.

I work away a lot and take care that I either go for a swim, a sauna or a long walk around the hotel to make a break from the office environment.

Whatever you do or choose to refer to, make sure it involves doing something constructive and worthwhile, and wherever possible focus on transferable skills.

Summary

Today focuses on all the dimensions that make you unique. It is your opportunity to be proud of your achievements and honest about where there is room for improvement. Feel free to talk about your ambitions and ideas for the future. They won't be used against you, they help to understand you as a person rather than just another job applicant.

Start to collect comments that people make about you and notice how you feel about yourself in a structured way. Create a portfolio of ideas that would fit into this part of the interview. Read through it regularly and think what it says about you. That way you will have material from which to select appropriately, whatever interview you attend.

Who are you?

- Present yourself confidently
- Write a profile statement and practise saying it
- Prepare for questions, which are about you the person
- Identify what makes you different – your unique selling point
- Think through your achievements
- Research how other people perceive you
- How do you relax?

Whilst today has been focused on what makes you tick, tomorrow is more work related: why do you want the job and how will you do it?

How will you do the job?

Yesterday we concentrated on giving the interviewer an impression of *who you are*. We hope that you are feeling more confident about the more intimate aspects of yourself. Today we will take this a step further. It is not just you or your skills, experience and knowledge that the interviewer is interested in, they are also interested in how these interrelate – *how do you do the job*. You may have experienced situations when you've planned something well – all the component parts are great – but when you mix them together, things go disastrously wrong. You may be a brilliant candidate, with all the essential and desirable characteristics and experience, but your interviewer may sense your methods of working do not mach those of your prospective boss or department. Where this type of conflict is not constructive, it can be costly.

Interviewer's objectives	Interviewee's objectives
• What is your management style?	• Articulate my style with examples
• What motivates you?	• Clearly state what I want from work
• How do you motivate others?	• Demonstrate how I manage my team
• How does this fit with the culture?	• Express how I could add value
• What blocks might you experience?	• Describe my fit and flexibility
• How does your style complement others?	• Show how my style complements others

Today we will guide you through the relevant questions:

- Why this job?
- What motivates you?
- What is your management style?
- How will you do the job?

Why this job?

Why do you want this job? is a predictable interview question. It may not be quite so direct but at some point during the interview it will emerge. Consider the different ways of answering it.

Because it . . .

- was advertised
- matches my skills
- is the right time to be moving
- appealed to me

I was . . .

- excited by the advertisement
- seeking a challenge
- planning my next move

The 'because it' column has more of the 'push' factors that we mentioned on Tuesday; the 'I was' column contains more of the 'pull' factors. There is only a slight difference in the response, but if you choose your words carefully you sound planned, focused and proactive.

This only becomes a tough question when you haven't thought through your response. Is it a question you have ever seriously asked yourself? This is a good opportunity to work out what makes a job appealing to you and what might lessen its attraction. We are suggesting three key areas for you to think about:

CURRENT JOB

PROSPECTIVE JOB

- identity
- values
- preferred environment.

Identity

We often frame our understanding of our identity around what we do, rather than who we are. This is why yesterday we took you through a step-by-step approach to understanding yourself. When you describe yourself to a stranger you may say: *I'm a team leader, a programmer, a manager.* Much of our status comes from our title. We like shorthand ways to describe ourselves but this only conveys a part of the picture – the what rather than the how. There is a huge difference between identifying yourself as a project manager or as the central coordinator for large-scale capital projects. Think through how you would respond to the following questions:

- How would you describe yourself?
- Who do you want to be when you are at work?
- Which are your favourite roles?

Companies have identities, too, and these give employees
and customers a clear idea of what to expect from them.
Where there is a strong figurehead as founder, that person
often incorporates their identity and values into the
organisation. Take care to check that the external identity
which attracts you to an organisation is applied to the staff
too. For example, it would be inconsistent of an educational
organisation to advocate strongly the importance of lifelong
learning whilst blocking its staff from attending development
courses for themselves. You should work on a snappy
response to the question *What kind of organisation do you want
to work with?* Think broader than *I want to work in
pharmaceuticals* or *I want to work in retailing* as there are many
companies to choose from. What differentiates them
surrounds the *how* questions – the way in which they achieve
their objectives. *I want to work in a company that recognises and
rewards a job well done.*

Values

Your values relate to what is important to you when you are
at work. A key value might be security. If this describes you,
then an organisation with a low staff turnover and good
pension may suit you. If you value variety, then a job that
sends you around the world to buy products may appeal to
you. It may be that what matters most to you is a sense of
'celebrity', and so the opportunity to represent your
organisation at a national level would be exciting and

stimulating. Conversely, if this doesn't fit, you will be thrown into panic, anxiety or sheer terror at the thought of working in that environment. Think through the answers to the following questions:

- What matters to you when you are at work?
- Why do you go to work?

Whatever your values, you will enjoy your job much more if they are matched at work.

Preferred environment

This refers to where you are and who you are with. The comfort and safety of your surroundings make a big difference to job satisfaction and achievement. Think about what effect different work environments have had on you and which aspects you would like in any future jobs. Is it important to be able to work in natural light or more significant to have your own desk or office? You may also want to consider any environmental factors, such as transport, housing and schooling that affects you and your family.

Now you have a clear idea of what you are looking for in a job, you can start to form some answers to the following questions.

Why do you want to work for us? What makes you think you're right for the job? What makes this the right job for you?

I want to work for an organisation that is committed to staff involvement at all levels. I know that you have installed a rigorous 360° appraisal scheme and that you have acted positively on the feedback you have received.

When I rang your department for the annual figures, I was impressed by the friendliness of the administrator I spoke to. I rang back for some fairly obscure data and felt that my request was treated seriously. That is just one example of the way I like to deal with people. I feel I would fit into this organisation.

In the examples above you are reinforcing how you do your job by talking about what you know about the organisation. In a very subtle way you have communicated aspects of yourself. At the same time, with this as with the following question, we would always advocate honesty.

What is most important to you in a job? What would make the ideal employer for you?

The most important aspect of a job is that I am able to work at my own pace and in my own space. I am a specialist in my commercial field and I have learned over the years to trust my intuition. My work is highly regarded throughout the industry and I wish to stay pre-eminent. It follows that my ideal employer would be someone prepared to nurture my creativity and appreciate my need for space. I enjoy working in organisations where my thoroughness is valued and appreciated.

Management styles

Management style has changed over the last decade. There are many terms used to describe recent management style, including the following:

- Coaching – let's find a solution together
- Organic – change as a process rather than event
- Empowerment – working with, accountability, responsibility
- Quality – how can we improve?
- Customer focus – listening, understanding, responding
- Learning company – acquiring new knowledge and skills

For most organisations, language such as *do as I say* is now abhorrent. Change is something which is embraced, rather than opposed, and the quality of working relationships is seen as the key to achievement. From your research you should have some idea about the organisation's style of management:

- How do they describe their management style?
- What do they refer to in their competencies?
- What do you pick up through their literature?

It is quite normal to have a series of questions about your management style. However, interviewers are not interested in your theoretical perspective but how you put the theory into practice. So prepare your answers. If you talk about empowerment, tell them how you do it and with what results.

What kind of people do you find it difficult to work with? How have you worked successfully with these difficult people?
Watch out for these! There could be an assumption that you have some difficulties in your people management skills. It would be foolish to suggest that you never have challenges with people. Here you need to demonstrate tact, understanding and diplomacy without being sidetracked into a lengthy discussion of certain types of people.

Everyone had lost patience with one member of the team who always came up with why something wasn't good enough or couldn't possibly work. When I spent some time with her and told her that it appeared as if she was always putting our ideas down, she was horrified. She explained that she thought the team was working brilliantly and she wanted to use her attention to detail as a final checkpoint. We agreed that she would point out all the positives she associated with our projects and we would give her five minutes at the end of every team meeting to air her concerns. After that no one could have hoped for a more committed team member.

You have been given a project that required you to interact at different levels within the organisation. How do you do this? What levels are you most comfortable with?
This is a two-part question that probes communication and self-confidence. The first part indirectly asks how you interact with senior staff and motivate those working with and for you on a project. The second part of the question is saying: *Tell me whom you regard as your peer group – help me categorise you.*

Which management thinker has influenced your practice?
Be honest with this question. If the answer is 'no one' then
state it. You may not be a great reader but something will
have influenced your practice. You could interpret this
question and talk about a manager you respect.

I have been most influenced by . . . their work had the most
significant effect on my understanding of how I could make the
difference and how I always needed to have my goal in mind.

I am not a great reader of management books. I have worked for
many people who have influenced my practice, and through
observation and discussion I have come to understand what goes on
in their heads, and I have applied this to myself.

You may also be asked for your definitions of terms such as:
'co-operation', 'management' etc. You should have some
definitions up your sleeve for this type of question. Avoid
sounding textbook-based and wherever possible give
examples.

Motivation

Questions about motivation are trying to uncover which
forces determine what you want and need from your
working life. These are sometimes referred to as 'drivers' and
are sources of energy and direction that become obvious as
people study the shape of their working lives. Research has
identified nine distinct career drivers that can act as key
motivators.

Key drivers	Seeking
Power/influence	To be in control of people and resources
Affiliation	To be part of the group, being popular
Expertise	A high level of accomplishment in a specialised field
Material rewards	Possessions, wealth and a high standard of living
Creativity	To innovate and be identified with original work
Autonomy	To be independent and able to make key decisions
Security	A solid and predictable future
Search for meaning	Doing things you believe are valuable for their own sake
Status	To be recognised, admired and respected

Adapted from Schein's career drivers

Take some time to think about which of these have motivated you in your career choices and decisions to date. How do they fit in with the opportunities offered by the types of jobs and organisations you are considering at present? Then think about the following set of questions.

What motivates you to put in your greatest effort at work?
What are the most important rewards you want from your career?

It is important to me that my work makes a positive contribution to the wider community. I want to work on issues that are important and do more than just promoting my career.

I want my products to have my 'name' on them and I want to be genuinely innovative in my work.

What was your least favourite position? What role did your boss play in your career at that point?
Here the interviewer is trying to uncover style-related issues, how you cope with a negatively-framed question and how you constructively criticise both your boss and the organisation. Be careful not to lay blame.

What I disliked most about my former company was the fact that it offered very little risk and reward. It was a very mature company with exceptionally long staff tenure. Working for the Sales Director had the most challenges. We worked very well together personally, but he needed to be much more proactive in terms of anticipating the workload. He prided himself in putting out fires. My style, conversely, was to forecast potential problems before they arose. It got very tiring after a while and took most of the fun out of coming to work every day.

You should also be prepared for questions along the lines of: *What is more important to you, pay or the type of job you are doing?* If you are applying for a job with a high element of commission, then you will do well with a 'materials reward' driver. If you are going for a more vocational type of job then 'search for meaning' or 'affiliation' is likely to be stronger.

Summary

Today, we have taken you through the questions relating to how you will do the job. We have given you some exercises to help you clarify and understand what matters to you at work and how you want to achieve it.

Why this job?

- Identity
- Values
- Environment

What is your management style?

- Theoretical understanding
- Examples of good practice

What motivates you?

- Your driving forces

Tomorrow you will be looking at one of the most difficult issues to define, that of fit.

Will you fit?

So you have convinced the interviewer that you can do the job. You have the necessary skills, knowledge, experience, training and, given the opportunity your behaviours, motivators, style and characteristics would help you do the job. The important question now is *Will you fit?*

Today, we will focus on convincing the interviewer that you will. The question of *fit* is being assessed from your very first exchange: from the style and language in your letter, your choice of clothes, your handshake, through to your degree of articulation and your understanding of the questions. Whilst this is, to some degree, a subconscious process, it is probably the most influential in decision making.

Will you fit?

- Scenarios
- How long will you stay?
- How much are you worth?
- How does this role fit?
- How do they fit? – your questions

This is a key area for the interviewer to get right. In the main, they want to recommend the appointment of someone who will benefit the organisation, work well with the existing staff and embrace the culture. Sometimes, of course, they want just the opposite. You may be applying for a job that involves reducing staffing and making a unit mean, lean and cost effective. If that is so, make sure it fits you.

The interviewer needs to achieve a good fit between the job role and the organisation's expectations. Someone with the personal and professional ability that matches the organisation's policies and management style. The better the fit, the more harmonious and effective the professional relationship.

THIS WILL BE YOUR OFFICE

Interviewer's objectives	Interviewee's objectives
• Do you fit the company image?	• Would I feel proud to be with this company?
• How will you adapt to the culture?	• Will I want to talk about where I work?
• Would our clients want you at their meetings?	• Will I wear the uniform with pride?
• Will you blend with the team?	• Do I feel comfortable here?
• Could you represent us?	• Could I represent them?

These are probably the most important questions for the interviewer to find answers to as a wrong decision can be costly to the organisation in terms of time, energy, lost opportunities, internal and external relationship breakdowns. This is the final balancing act for the interviewer.

You must have been exposed to someone in your career who didn't fit, so you will understand at first hand what this feels like and the disruption it can cause. Therefore, the judgement of fit is the part of the interview process that interviewers are most cautious about. There are some sophisticated questions and situations that have been devised to gauge fit, but much of this part of the process remains instinctive. Decisions are often made on a 'gut' reaction or discussions that rest on perception rather than evidence. If there is ever a part of the process that interviewers will discuss at length, disagree on and even get second opinions on, it is fit.

In some cases it is obvious: the interviewer will know you will fit. Sometimes, they may make comments such as:

- . . . there was something about them . . .
- . . . I'm sure they could do the job . . .
- . . . I can't put my finger on it . . . or even
- . . . I'm not sure how they would fit . . .

As fit is so difficult to gauge, companies have devised their own sets of questions to help uncover whether your style, manner and character match theirs.

Case history: One of the companies we advised was receiving many complaints about the style and attitude of a senior manager. He was rude and unfeeling, with no interest in staff concerns. When he was employed, this organisation was overstaffed and running at a loss. He was brought in to stop the downward spiral. There was no room for sentiment and he achieved his objectives. Once the rot had stopped, his skills were inconsistent with the organisation's needs. Eventually he moved on to another 'troubleshooting' job. He no longer fitted in and rather than change his style, he moved on – a pattern he will often follow.

Scenarios

Increasingly, interviewers are making use of real life, relevant situations to check how you fit with their organisation. Most of the colleagues we talked to agreed that their most challenging and revealing questions were ones which asked the candidate to declare how they would react in a given scenario.

What would you do? questions can fall into two categories: hypothetical or real. They focus on how you would cope. The interviewer does not want to hear the answer *it depends* – they already know that. They want to know how you process information, what your first actions would be, who you would talk to . . . the list goes on. You have to think on your feet and put yourself in the interviewer's shoes. The context of their question should give you some understanding of what are they interested in so you can give them what they are looking for.

It's 8.00 a.m., your most prestigious client is due to arrive at 9.00 a.m. and the computer equipment for your presentation hasn't arrived. What do you do?

I think we've all faced situations like this. I always try to plan against anything like this happening by setting up presentations in advance and not leaving things to chance. But given this situation I would have the contact numbers for the people bringing the equipment. Then I could contact them and, if necessary, arrange for other equipment to be delivered.

What would you do? questions often bring a similar level of anxiety as the real situations. Don't slip into the easy trap of saying *panic* in reply. You may be thinking that, and many of these situations do create a level of anxiety, but remember your interviewer wants to hear how you would cope, what you would do and how you would deliver given the uncertainty and ambiguity that happens in everyday situations.

Every company has its own quirks. How dysfunctional was your last company, and how would you deal with a company's shortcomings and inconsistencies?
When we came across this question, from sample questions used by a large multinational company, it stopped us in our tracks. Remember, this is a *What would you do?* question. Beware of these questions as they are there to test your ability to remain objective and positive about your last organisation, and your interpretation of dysfunction – what it means to you, how you tackle organisational development issues. The list is endless, but your answer must remain succinct – so think carefully.

My last company was open about its dysfunctionality as it was the flip side of its effectiveness. The passion with which it attacked the business created a high degree of emotion in all functions. This led to a need to react very quickly when messages or changes were interpreted wrongly to prevent them spiralling out of control. In one case, for example, I called everyone to a short meeting to explain what had and hadn't already been decided by senior management.

You are chairing the monthly interdepartmental meeting. All is going well – except for the head of operations, a bright and ambitious woman. She keeps looking at her watch, sighing and whispering 'hurry up' when someone else speaks. Eventually she cracks and suggests you speed the meeting up – she has places to go, people to see.

I would want to tackle this in two ways. Firstly at the meting by acknowledging her urgency and asking for her patience to listen to all contributions. I would also remind her of our agreed timings and that we would finish on time. My next step would be to talk to her alone outside the meeting, challenge her behaviour and ask for her ideas about reaching a workable solution.

Your success in answering all the *What would you do?* questions is to think about the interviewer's objectives and respond to these directly. Be honest, succinct, direct and help them understand how this relates to you generally.

How long will you stay?

Whilst interviewers have a current need, they will also be thinking about the future. The investment in the interview process or in consultant costs needs to demonstrate some return. So the questions which relate to how long will you stay or what you want to do next are important to the interviewer. A good fit is likely to encourage you to stay, and be a greater return on the investment.

How long will you stay with the organisation?
If the interviewer asks this question, they may be thinking of offering you a job. So build on this. You may want to end your answer with a question of your own that really puts the ball back in the interviewer's court.

I would really like an opportunity to make a contribution to the success of the organisation and could see where I could add value. I can operationalise strategies and love to learn. As long as I am growing professionally and challenged, there is no reason for me to make a move. How long do you think I would be challenged here?

■ F R I D A Y ■

Where do you see yourself in ten years time?
Questions such as this don't require you to make a long-term commitment to the organisation. They are probing your career ambitions and goals. Most managers would be expected to have thought through their career plans so that they could at least articulate a goal, although it is surprising how few can. This question is difficult to answer in terms of a role, but it's not asking that. It's asking you to consider where do you see yourself in terms of responsibilities, contribution to an organisation, work style etc.

Ten years ought to give me time to grow within an organisation like yours which provides the right nourishment, such as training and good management. I am ambitious and would be keen to reach my full potential which would be . . .

You may want to add: *It is reasonable to expect that other exciting opportunities will crop up in the meantime and I am always keen to apply my skills in different environments.*

The question may also be asked in the following way:

How would this post fit into your long-term career plans?

My plans have always been influenced by experiences and opportunities. I believe this post would be just right. I could use the skills I have developed and be sufficiently challenged to develop whilst learning from new people, processes and clients. I could then look forward to what opportunities my success in this role would bring.

How much do you think you are worth?

It is not uncommon to be asked to put a price on your head. You can quantify worth in many ways:

- The value you add
- Your market value
- What you are paid at the moment, or
- How much the organisation is prepared to pay

Our advice would be start with a high figure and don't be afraid of negotiation. Many people find they undersell themselves because they are not ready for such a direct question, so don't fall into that trap. Be bold. It is not unreasonable to ask for 10–20% more than your current package – always quantify all your benefits: discounts, healthcare, pension, car allowance, shares, etc. when negotiating salary, as these could be worth more than you imagine.

What salary do you require?

I am looking for something in the range of £x–£y. You don't need to go into any more detail than this. Do not answer this question with a question, such as *How much are you prepared to pay?*

How does this role fit?

You may be faced with questions you feel are only asked of you because of your gender, disability, ethnicity or sexual orientation. These are some of the more difficult questions to deal with as they challenge your fit, not on the basis of skills, experience or behaviour but because of who you are. The key to these questions is to understand the reason they are asked.

In the interviewee's seat it may feel as if you are being discriminated against; in the interviewer's seat it may be they genuinely want to know if you are a good person in whom to invest their time, training and money.

Keeping the interviewer's underlying question in mind, you will have some guidelines on how to answer. If you want the job, then you have to answer the question in a way that says: *yes, I am a good bet or a low risk.*

This style of question is disappearing, but every so often you will be faced with one that can 'wobble' you, not just for the duration of the question but beyond. You may also want to consider whether you would want to work for an employer that asks such questions as:

- What is your marital status?
- Are you in a long-term relationship?
- Whom do you live with?
- Do you plan to have a family? When?
- How many children do you have?
- What are your childcare arrangements?

For example, in response to the question: *What are your childcare arrangements?* you may choose to respond: *If you are asking would I be willing and able to travel as needed by the job, the answer is 'yes', I would just need some notice to make the necessary arrangements . . . I am willing to work overtime and have often stayed late to complete tasks.* This can come across better than a direct: *Would you ask that question of a man?*

Also, don't be surprised if you are asked for your birth certificate, passport, proof of qualifications, or any document containing your national insurance number. Legislative changes require employers to establish that each new employee, at whatever level, can legally work in the country. Every employee, even those at the most senior level, should be asked to produce evidence.

Do they fit? – your questions

The last time you bought a car or a house, did you ask about the financing, have it valued or investigate its reliability? We would hope that you did! We would suggest that your next carer move is at least as important. So if you want to impress your potential manager with your grasp of the position and knowledge of the organisation, it makes sense to draw up a list of questions. Asking good questions at an interview helps you get the information you need to make an intelligent decision; it also shows the interviewer that you've done your homework and are in a position to discuss the job's potential opportunities and challenges. Here are just a few questions you may want to think of asking:

Organisation

- What are the long-range plans?
- I consider your competitors to be . . . what do you think?
- What did you wish you knew about the organisation before you started?
- What values are sacred to the organisation?
- How are decisions made?
- What is the organisation's philosophy towards employees?

Success and measurement

- Could you give me examples of the best results the previous holders of this position have attained?
- What is your biggest problem and what role would I have in solving it?

Development opportunities

- What opportunities of advancement are there for me?
- How are staff developed from this post?
- Why did this post become vacant?

The interviewer

- What are your key selection criteria for the post?
- How long have you worked here? In what capacities?
- How do you allocate and review work?

Asking articulate and well-thought-through questions leaves a good impression on your interviewer. It's a great opportunity to professionally challenge the interviewer and be remembered. Try to avoid going over old information and remember this is not the appropriate place to talk through terms and conditions – this leaves the interviewer with the impression that this is all you are interested in.

Summary

Today we have addressed the issue of *fit*. The interviewer wants to find out if you are the right person for the job not just in terms of what you can do but how you do it. You also want to assess how they and the organisation fit your needs and requirements.

- How could you fit into their scenarios?
- Are you a worthwhile investment?
- Do they meet your requirements?

So far this week we have developed your understanding of how to respond to tough interview questions. Tomorrow we will help you put the finishing touches to your preparation by focusing on you.

Are you ready?

At this stage of the week we expect you to feel more confident about tackling tough interview questions. Only you will understand what makes you feel supremely confident. We have attempted to prepare you by looking at the interview from different perspectives. Perhaps the most important perspective is to put yourself in the shoes of the interviewer, to understand their motives for asking the questions, and to respond appropriately. Remember, your interviewer thinks you can do the job and they want to help you bring your application to life.

Today is about bringing all your preparation together and harnessing all your inner resources to ensure that you are ready and raring to go when the next interview arrives.

Are you ready?

- Rehearsing your responses
- Preparing your thoughts
- Focussing on your outcome
- Relaxing before the event
- Is this the job for you?
- Tackling tough interview questions

We have focused throughout the week on your responses to tough interview questions. Preparing what you are going to say and how you are going to say it are equally important.

Have you ever been in a situation in which you've wanted to listen to someone because they know their subject or you respect their opinions? Try as you might, you've been unable to give them your full attention. Their delivery has undermined the message. This could happen to you, too. You can prevent this happening to you by spending time rehearsing. Prepare yourself so that every aspect of what you say convinces and engages your audience.

Your objectives

- Get myself as ready as I can
- Put all my preparation into practice
- Imagine and rehearse my success
- Draw on and recognise all my resources

Rehearsing your responses

What makes a great performance? Whatever the context in which you practice sport, art, craft, business, there are some essential components: skill, understanding the criteria for success, practice and learning. The interview is just the same. Whilst our comments this week have focused on developing your skills and understanding the criteria for success, do not underestimate the importance of practice, feedback and learning.

Saying your responses out loud, asking a trusted friend to be your interviewer, working with a coach, taping yourself, can all help. Physically saying the words will give you a sense of their impact, as some of your answers may look better than they sound! Rehearsal takes planning and effort, so be sure to give yourself time and don't be put off by the fact that it may be embarrassing. It's better to be embarrassed in front of a colleague or friend, where the cost is personal, than in front of the interviewer where the cost may include prospects and earning potential. We like the notion: *The more I practice the luckier I get*, a response golfer Gary Player made to a shout of *lucky shot*.

Often, a bad day experience, when broken down into its component parts, does not seem so bad after all. A bad experience can affect you and it can leave you expecting the worst to happen. This can send your self-esteem plummeting, with far reaching consequences. If you're struggling with some of these thoughts, you need to exorcise them by exposing them to the light of rational thought. Balance your thoughts on what could go wrong with what will go right. When you think positively, you behave positively and it shows.

The following questions may help your rehearsal:

	Worst interview to date	**Best interview to date**
How did you prepare?	....	....
What did you feel about the job?	....	....
What did you notice on arrival?	....	....
What did you do well?	....	....
What could you have done differently?	....	....

Preparing your thoughts

Many of our comments this week have been based on logical, practical and analytical assumptions. Some commentators refer to this as 'left brain' activity. Whilst it's likely that much of an interview will also be based there, remember the other side, your right brain activity. This is the source of your imagination and creativity. Your ability to demonstrate your creativity is as important to your success. It's part of your uniqueness. You can also harness your imagination to create the interview in which you feel at your best.

Think for a moment about the notion of beginner's luck. No one has told them how difficult it is to succeed and they have no prior memory of doing it well or badly. In fact if they believe in beginner's luck, they will expect to do well the first time. Then, depending on their beliefs, they go on and build on their success – or they become gradually worse. Our ability to achieve excellence or perform well is dependent on how well we believe we can do.

Poor performers

- It was a fluke
- It won't last
- I always mess up

Good performers

- I can make this a success
- I can keep doing this well
- I always do well

You can make or break an interview just by talking to yourself in the above way. You know what you say to yourself and how to mentally prepare yourself for the task ahead. We would recommend the following:

- encourage yourself
- tell yourself you can do it
- think about previous successes
- focus on what success could bring

It may help you to develop affirmations: short, positively-focused statements that introduce and reinforce the way you want to be. They are always stated in the present or present continuous tense as if they already exist. They work on the premise that thoughts create experience and keep the mind programmed in the positive. As you repeat them regularly, so you will believe them and your mind will focus on what you want.

Write and repeat your own affirmations about the interview and the new post you are aiming for:

Example affirmations:

- I always do well at interview
- I enjoy the opportunity to tackle tough interview questions
- Everyday brings a new and welcome challenge.

Also remind yourself that the interviewer doesn't hold all the trump cards. Put yourself in their shoes and you'll realise that they have as much at stake in the interview as you. What if they appoint the wrong person? They are probably under as much pressure as you are because they can't afford to make a bad decision.

Focus on your outcome

There are examples from many walks of life which suggest that if you focus on your outcome and imagine yourself having succeeded or being successful you will achieve whatever you set out to achieve. Setting goals focuses your attention and action. With clear goals you are more likely to engage in purposeful behaviour. When you know what you want, you are more likely to pursue it. With realistic and specific goals you know what you are aiming for; with no goals you have no target.

So start this process by thinking what you want your outcome to be and create some affirmations to achieve it.

Exercise

- Find a place where you can sit or lie down for a few uninterrupted minutes.
- Close your eyes and create your ideal interview.
- Start from the night before. See and feel yourself relaxed and sleeping well.
- Wake up feeling energetic and keen to be there.
- Imagine yourself arriving for the interview.
- Feel calm and confident as you enter the building.
- Tell yourself how well prepared you are and ready to enjoy the interview.
- You are treated with respect and feel comfortable.
- You know you are performing well.
- Experience the interview going the way you want.
- See yourself leave the interview with a sense of satisfaction and achievement.
- Open your eyes and enjoy your positivity.

Relaxing before the event

We would encourage everyone reading this book to take or create some form of relaxation before an interview. How you relax is your choice. You will know what works for you. For some this may mean activity: a visit to the gym, swimming, a round of golf, gardening, walking the dog. For others it may mean inactivity, stopping the round of activities which make up a normal day and spending time with family, friends or partners. Or taking time on your own to read, listen to music, write letters or do nothing. What maters is that you do something that relaxes you.

When you are relaxed and not overly tired, you are much more able to deal with situations as they emerge. You are much less likely to make mistakes as you will be alert. Your words and actions will support rather than contradict each other. Also decide how you approach the interview, otherwise all your preparation and relaxation would be in vain. Picture the two scenes below:

Scene 1	Scene 2
• Work until midnight the night before	• Complete preparation the previous day
• Haven't received a map	• Ring to check details – location
• Decide to set off, will ring on approach	• Decide to travel by train
• Arrive in town with just 15 minutes to spare	• Plan to arrive with hour to spare
• Car park is 10 minute walk	• Have lunch on site
• A queue at security of 20 people	• Meet employees, talk about company

Which scene would you prefer? Just reading Scene 1 can raise your anxiety. Imagine how you would fare walking into an interview with that as your build up. Creating your own Scene 2 is not about luck, it is down to planning and preparation and if you want to do well, don't leave it to chance! We would encourage you to leave time to relax and not to be distracted by tasks or people. This time is important to your success.

Is this the job for you?

As we saw yesterday, the fit issue affects both parties. You may be ideal for the company, but are they the perfect match for you?

Will they

- support your development?
- look good on your CV?
- offer good prospects for the future?
- fit with your style?

Will the job

- be sufficiently challenging?

How will you

- complement the team?
- add value?

If your answers to any of the above questions are not clear then you should check your goals and motivation. One of the major factors that can influence whether the job is for you will be your relationship with your boss. We would recommend that you never accept a position without an interview with your immediate manager. No one has more impact on your career. Their performance, feedback, attitude, expectations and style will have an effect on your performance and the way you feel about your job. In turn, their conversations with their boss can colour higher management's long term perceptions of you.

Before you accept a job, get to know your boss. Ask probing questions:

- What are the key indicators of success for you in this role?
- What do you expect from me personally?
- How could I influence you?
- How would I know your opinion of my performance?
- How would you describe your style?

You need to determine whether your work styles, goals and philosophies are compatible. Decide if this is someone you could admire. If they prove not to be, perhaps you should look for another job, managed by a person who more closely mirrors your image of a good manager.

By reading company literature, and by active listening, you can uncover what their values are. By looking at pictures or examples used when answering your questions, you will get a feel of how the company likes to see itself. One word of caution: if you find yourself at variance with your potential employer's value system, you would do well to consider any job offer very carefully. It is difficult to be successful in a culture in which you feel an outsider. If you sense that the fit is not right from your perspective, then we would suggest that you don't pursue the opportunity. If the company is embarking on a major change, be sure of where the motivation and commitment for the change comes from. Are you being appointed as one of the change agents? There is nothing more de-skilling than being in a company where you don't fit and there should be signs of this almost immediately. If your gut reaction tells you no, listen to it and try to analyse why.

If you think you are close to a job offer that you want to accept, this may be the time to talk about the practicalities. Even if you don't discuss these in the interview, they are worth considering when you are negotiating from the strong position of having a job offer.

Practicalities

- Will you need a medical?
- Preferred start date
- Pension details
- Salary review – independent of appraisal, how often?
- Private healthcare scheme
- Car scheme details
- Insurance company and personal
- Expected job and company growth
- Potential career paths
- Leave allocation
- Profit sharing

Tackling interview questions

This week was designed to give you an insight into the world of the selection interview. An interview is a discussion with a clear purpose: the interviewer wants to know how you will bring benefits to them and the company. They are seeking someone who can fill a vacancy with minimum upheaval. You want a new job, a new challenge or a change. You also want to get there as calmly as possible.

Our advice throughout the week relates to the preparation and thought required to develop a script for your answers. But remember, if you are too staged in your responses then your interviewer will detect this. The words you use need to be yours, not ours, or they will sound affected and unconvincing. Of course the interviewer wants to know that you are taking the process seriously and have done the necessary preparation. They also want to know how you deal with the unexpected and how you might respond in the real world where not everything goes according to plan. Remember to think of your interview as a discussion rather than a test. Even if a panel of people interview you, they are only asking one question at a time. That is what you need to concentrate on.

Tackling tough interviews

- Identify your tough questions
- Establish rapport with everyone you meet
- Your education, skill and competencies
- You and your personality
- What makes you tick?
- What would you do if . . .?
- Prepare creatively

We wish you well in whatever types of interview you attend. You can now go to them knowing you are prepared and that you have all the resources you need to answer whatever you are asked. Now you've read the book, you should be saying:

Tough questions? I don't know what you mean!

INform Training and Communication provides a professional client-centred range of services. To find out more visit www.inform-global.com